MOTI
INTERVIEWING
FOR
CAMPUS
POLICE

By David J Closson, M.S.

Copyright © 2015 <DJC Solutions LLC>
All rights reserved.
ISBN: 978-09967985-0-1
ISBN-10: 0996798501

ABOUT THE AUTHOR

David Closson is the Assistant Director of the Illinois Higher Education Center (I.H.E.C.) where he provides professional development, consultation and trainings for the institutes of higher education throughout Illinois. The mission of I.H.E.C. is to reduce negative health and safety consequences to Illinois college students related to alcohol, other drugs and violence. He previously worked as the Crime Prevention Officer, Field Training Officer and Patrol Officer for the Eastern Illinois University Police Department. He spent time working as a Corrections Officer and prior to that was a Sergeant in the Illinois Army National Guard. He was deployed as a part of Operation Iraqi Freedom. After spending a year in Iraq with his infantry unit and his recon team, he was awarded two Army Commendation Medals, one for valor and one for meritorious service and a Combat Infantryman's Badge.

David is an Eastern Illinois University alumni (2008 & 2013) with a BS in Biology and a MS in Technology, Training and Development. His master's degree work focused on motivational interviewing for campus police. He has presented to and trained nearly 9,000 people on topics ranging from military tactics, law enforcement patrol operations, verbal communication techniques, motivational interviewing, bystander intervention, alcohol/drug safety, sexual assault prevention and conflict resolution.

You can contact David via email at
Dave@daveclosson.com
www.DaveClosson.com
www.MIforCampusPolice.com
Facebook.com/DaveClosson
Twitter: @Dclosn

This book is dedicated to my family.
Without their love and support this book would
not be possible.

A thank you to the law enforcement officers
across America.

TABLE OF CONTENTS

FOREWORD

Any law enforcement officer who reads this book on "Motivational Interviewing" will find him/herself in a win-win situation. The book is a quick read and will motivate the reader to peruse the material quickly in order to get to the end where there are examples to assist in the implementation of "Motivational Interviewing" (MI). Although the book is geared towards campus police officers the material and concept is beneficial to all law enforcement. If one considers the situation now involving law enforcement personnel and the public, an officer would be truly missing a chance to not only defuse a potential physical situation but also develop new and improved lines of communication with the public (albeit one at a time!) An officer can never have too many "sources of information" on the street and this book will help the officer in developing and maintaining those contacts. The public can/will develop an enhanced and positive image of law enforcement if MI is tried at an appropriate time and then followed up on. I commend the author for promoting this concept. After all as he says "you can always do police work" but if the timing is appropriate and the subject is rational then the officer can use MI to his/her advantage and not only assist an individual in time of potential arrest but also develop the sources of information for the future.

-Terry Lucas

Terry Lucas is a 43 year veteran of state and federal law enforcement who also enjoyed a 28 year career as an officer in the US Army and the Illinois National Guard. Lucas served with the US Department of Justice throughout the nation and also volunteered to serve with a small Department of Justice mission in Iraq which assisted in the trial of Sadaam Hussein. Lucas currently serves on the Executive Board of the FBI National Academy Association as the National Historian.

SECTION I

Introduction

The smoke that hung in the hallway was strong enough to burn my eyes. I knocked on the door and braced myself for the inevitable confrontation that I knew was about to take place. On the other side of the door there was the sound of a drawer being slammed shut, and then the door opened. I was almost knocked off my feet by the over-whelming smell of cannabis. The young man gazed up at me, along with my fellow officer, with unfocused eyes. We had been dispatched to his room because of a complaint from fellow students. Truth be told, this person already had a few previous interactions with the police in regards to drug use, so this was familiar territory for both of us. As a police officer at Eastern Illinois University, I had been trained to deal with these types of occurrences. But what happened that night was different. I chose this time to take an overall student-centered approach, rather than approach the issue head on.

When I was a sergeant in the Illinois Army National Guard (infantry), I was deployed to Iraq in 2005. I led more than 180 combat patrols, and my recon team was the most successful in the entire battalion. We led daily patrols through the city streets, where we interacted and built relationships with the Iraqi civilians. Our ability to build relationships and work with the civilians led us to be very successful. The civilians turned to us for help and gave us all kinds of information leading to hidden weapons and the location of insurgents. I saw the success of community policing in a war zone and its ability to cross cultural barriers. I would later apply this community policing approach as a college police officer.

After returning stateside, I had the opportunity to work as a corrections officer at the Douglas County Sheriff's Office. This is where I was first exposed to the book *Verbal Judo*,[1] and I quickly saw the importance of tactical communications. In the jail we didn't have firearms or a ton of officers for backup. I worked the midnight shift and since it was a small jail, I was often the only one working there. Backup was far away, so I was

[1] Thompson, George J., and Jerry B. Jenkins. *Verbal Judo: The Gentle Art of Persuasion.* Rev. ed. New York: Quill, 2004.

forced to rely on my verbal communication. Between making rounds through the cell blocks, I would read *Verbal Judo* and Dale Carnegie's book, *How to Win Friends and Influence People*.[2] I saw several overlaps with these two books, including themes such as respect, empathy and don't be a jerk! I thought to myself, "Hey, I've got a captive audience here. Let's practice." I got to know the inmates' personalities and found out which ones were trouble and which ones were not. Then I would read, learn and then practice!

I was hired as a police officer at Eastern Illinois University in 2010 and put a pause on pursuing my master's degree while I attended the University of Illinois Police Training Institute.

I spent three months training at the Police Academy and three months at EIU under a field training officer (FTO). I followed my FTO on patrol and quickly began applying the lessons learned in Iraq — balancing community policing while not jeopardizing safety. My reputation spread and I was asked to apply for the crime prevention officer position in January of 2012. In March I was chosen for the position. In building a team across campus to expand the reach of crime prevention, I began to work closely with the

---

[2] Carnegie, Dale. *How to Win Friends & Influence People*. Rev. ed. New York: Pocket Books, 1998.

director of the student standards office, Dr. Heather Webb. We both thought it would be a good idea to get the police department involved in the prevention and education side of alcohol and drug use on campus along with also being a part of the sanctioning efforts.

I really enjoyed working with the students in this manner. At the end of the sanction classes the students always said, "Wow this wasn't what I was expecting. I was expecting death by Power-Point and just being lectured to." In this class we applied many of the skills needed for motivational interviewing (MI), such as open-ended questions, affirmations, reflections, summaries and overall critical thinking. This class reinforced my MI skills, but as I saw the overlap of fundamental skills and techniques, I began to think about where else these skills could be applied.

The student's reactions and the success of the sanctioning classes, the versatility of the skills from my grad school classes, the importance of verbal judo/communication learned from Iraq, and working in the jail and patrolling as a police officer gave me an idea. I began to research and learn more about MI and why it worked. Then just as I did at the jail, I practiced!

As I stood outside that student's door, I realized I had a golden opportunity to put those various techniques into play. I decided to use the MI methods to see if those would help. At first, this student expressed ambivalence toward change. He said that he enjoyed smoking and that it helped him relax. On the other hand he said it isn't good for him and he is also getting in a lot of trouble. We then talked about his ambivalence toward smoking. We didn't move through all of the stages of change, but he really began thinking about why he should change his behavior. I began to ask questions to strengthen his own internal motivation to change. The conversation flowed so naturally that it surprised me (actually, I think both of us were a bit taken aback!). I did empathize with the student. I felt for his struggle and wanted him to succeed in changing his ways. This is very important!

The area director, Jessica Ward, was on the scene, as this took place in one of the buildings she supervised. She knew the student from his previous dealings with police and housing staff. After we were done talking with the student, she came to me and said something that I can still hear today. She said she had never seen a police officer take such an interest in a student, care about them and take time to talk to them in that way. She was amazed!

Things really started to click in my mind. The way the interaction made me feel, the feedback from

Ms. Ward, how the MI style naturally fit and the reaction from the student all told me this needed to be shared.

Each fall, as a new school year begins, colleges and universities are flooded with students. While these people come from all walks of life, they do have one thing in common: they all want to get the most out of their college experience. For so many of these students, this will be their first real opportunity to be away from home (read: finally, a chance to party!). These students will be ready to explore their independence, try out new skills and push their boundaries.

After a while, hearing the same message over and over again about the dangers of alcohol can start to sound like Charlie Brown's teacher droning on. But the truth is, it's a very real problem that remains on the rise. You don't need to look any further than your own campus to find examples of drinking or drugs and the danger and misery they bring to your school.

The following National Institute on Alcohol Abuse and Alcoholism[3] (N.I.A.A.A.) statistics relate to college students between the ages of 18 and 24:

Injury and death

- An estimated 1,825 students die yearly of unintended alcohol-related accidents, including motor vehicle accidents.
- Another 599,000 will be seriously injured.
- More than 150,000 students suffer from drinking-related health problems.
- 1.2 to 1.5% of students attempt suicide on account of drinking or drug use.
- 54% of binge drinkers have experienced significant memory loss at least once in the last year.

Assaults and Sexual Assaults

- 400,000 students annually report engaging in un-protected sex while under the influence.
- Of those, 100,000 report being too intoxicated to remember giving consent.
- 696,000 students are assaulted by another student who's been drinking.
- 97,000 students are the victims of alcohol-related sexual assault or rape.

---

[3] "College Drinking." National Institute on Alcohol Abuse and Alcoholism. 2015. Accessed January 7, 2015.

DUIs and Other Vehicular Offenses

- 3.36 million students report having driven under the influence.
- 30% of students who drank in the past year admitted to driving after drinking alcohol in the past 30 days.
- About one-half of all fatal car crashes among 18- to 24-year-olds are alcohol related.

You've heard these stories and seen many of these situations play out in real life, just as I have. I wrote this book to serve as a blueprint for you to follow as you go through the process of policing on campus. My goal was to pack this book full of information and tools but also to create a guide that is a quick and engaging read. Ultimately, this book is meant to be read not just once, but to become something you re-read and reference often as you move beyond theory into the truly transformative application of motivational interviewing.

As you read, remember what it was that brought these students to your college in the first place: they're looking to build a bright future for themselves. With this book, you can help! Given the right tools, you can help them be smart and live above the influence. Now let's begin...

SECTION II

College Drinking Behavior

There are two ways to look at alcohol consumption — by frequency and by quantity. What I have been seeing on campus is that most students don't drink frequently, yet when they do drink it is at a high quantity. A smaller percentage of the students will do both, frequent and in high quantity. These students who don't drink frequently, but in high quantity will naturally see less of the negative consequences of drinking and thus be more willing to accept drinking heavily on the weekends as a normal part of college.

In general, college students do not see anything wrong with their own drinking habits, but are quick to identify those self-destructive habits in others. The truth is, students are far less concerned with their drinking behavior than the campus administration is. I often hear from students that they already know everything they need to about alcohol and drinking.

The students — no matter what year in school — say that alcohol education programs should be for others and not for themselves. Seniors say it's best for freshmen, whereas freshmen say it is best for high school students and so forth.

When asking students if their drinking behaviors are a problem, the students say they would not consider them problems unless they occurred frequently. There are also misconceptions about the drinking norms across campus. This leads students to be more accepting of risky drinking behavior. Taking a look into social psychology research, students view their own problems as situation specific, whereas the problems of others are behavioral.[1] The social aspects of college often revolve around alcohol with their own customs. Dating situations are typically structured around alcohol, and certain social groups with high drinking reputations are often regarded with a high social status.[1]

Dating in college can be quite a challenge — and that's after you've gotten someone to agree to go out with you! When it comes to dinner out and a movie, fine dining is a real stretch on a student's budget. The two-for-one drinks and all-you-can-

[1] Walters, Scott T., and John Samuel Baer. *Talking with College Students about Alcohol: Motivational Strategies for Reducing Abuse.* New York: Guilford Press, 2006.

eat appetizers at the local watering hole can start to look pretty good. So what if you have to begin the evening's festivities at 4pm in order to get a head start on the cheap beer and stale pretzels. Plus, that's where all of your friends will be hanging out anyway...let the games begin!

My role of crime prevention officer entailed giving presentations to student groups, and I would estimate that to date, I have presented to more than 7,400 students. During these presentations, I often ask the students to share some safe drinking tips with me. Each time, they recite the list of common-sense safe drinking tips, showing that they have the knowledge, but choose to not follow it. They can easily identify dangerous drinking behavior in others but are slow to see it in themselves. Yet when they "over serve" themselves, they chalk it up to being part of the normal experience.

Picture this: three young men enter a bar and from the looks of it, they've already started to party. In fact, our trio is in full celebration mode, fresh off of a hard-fought victory at a beer pong championship. They are hoping to parlay that warm buzz into a full-fledged night on the town. Is one beer enough for these guys? Nah—they order the house special: a tower of beer that holds close to four pitchers of the golden ale.

Eager to get started on their battle with the tower, they go in search of a table. When they finally find an empty table in the back, they notice that in fact, there is already someone sitting there. Lying there, to be more precise, as the guy is obviously passed out drunk. The men look at each other and scoff, "What a loser — this guy is wasted!" Do they stop to take note of the fact that they themselves have already consumed just this evening more alcohol than most people drink in a weekend? Or that they are looking down their nose at someone who is drunk, when they are just about to drink four pitchers of beer?

College students are hypocrites when it comes to identifying risk/danger and drinking behavior. They may show up to the bar at 9pm and upon meeting a friend who is already sloppy drunk, label that friend as "having issues," when they will in fact be just as drunk later that night, or they were in the same situation the previous weekend. In addition, they are under the misconception that this behavior is perfectly acceptable as part of the overall college experience. It is in this combination that you can focus your attention; using the students' own knowledge to help them identify the problems and build their own motivation for change.

> *"Insanity: doing the same thing over and over again and expecting different results."* — *Albert Einstein*

Leading into the solution we must first briefly look at how college students learn.

Experiential Learning

Learning isn't a one-time event; it occurs in a cycle. More specifically, it is referred to as experiential learning, and it occurs in four stages. To start the cycle, there must be an immediate or concrete experience, which then provides the basis for reflections and observations. To continue the cycle, those observations are then used to develop new concepts for action. The final stage in the cycle is actively testing the new concepts. As the learner moves through the cycle, learning and behavior change takes place. The heart of learning is in the powerful reflections on concrete experiences. Understanding and applying the experiential learning cycle to college policing can lead to behavior change and future crime prevention!

Learning in everyday life is often overlooked as it is done automatically and subconsciously. Although theories of learning may seem complicated, experiential learning is simply when we have an experience and ask ourselves a few questions.

Think back to when you were a rookie cop: wide-eyed and conducting your first traffic stop scenario at the police academy. You likely had a few things you could have/should have done differently. After that first jumbled attempt, you thought about what happened and went over the scene in your mind. Maybe the conversation in your head went something like this:

"Man, I can't believe I said, 'You blew that stop sign' to the female driver. She really went off and took that as a sexual remark! What should I have done differently? Oh yeah, follow the traffic stop script the instructors taught us. 'Hi my name is Officer ____, with the _____ police department. The reason I stopped you today is because you failed to come to a complete stop at the stop sign at ___ street and ___ street. Is there a justified reason for this?' Next time I am going to use this script so the lady won't go off on me and I won't embarrass myself in front of the others."

Boom! That right there is experiential learning in its simplest form. Something happened to you. You thought about what happened and why it happened, and then came up with a new approach.

In regards to law enforcement, we often explain the consequences and what is expected. If someone chooses to break the law, we arrest them or assign the appropriate sanctions. This method of law enforcement keeps us removed from the change process.

As police officers we try to reduce criminal behavior, and if it does occur, we handle it. If we deter a crime from happening, that is considered success. However, deterring a crime does not necessarily encourage a change in behavior. There are many different reasons why a person may comply with a directive from a police officer. It may be to avoid jail or avoid paying a fine, or they may have seen the negative impact their behavior can have on their future. It is this latter reason that I want to focus on: compliance that will lead to a change (for the better!) in behavior. This will in turn reduce future criminal activity and have a positive effect on a variety of issues.

"The threat of punishment mostly teaches people how to avoid being punished in the future."[2] Punishment can gain short-term compliance, which is needed in law enforcement, but if law enforcement wants to support long-term behavior

---

[2] Walters, Scott T. *Motivating Offenders to Change a Guide for Probation and Parole*. Washington, DC: U.S. Dept. of Justice, National Institute of Corrections, 2007.

change, we must become an active part of the change process. Not only will this reduce criminal behavior; it will have a positive effect on many issues, such as:

- Creating and maintaining a safer community
- Improving police / community relations and the police department public image (here to help, not to arrest — i.e., the negative attention departments are getting now)
- Lowering high-risk drinking behavior and associated crimes
- Fulfillment in knowing as an officer of the law that we are helping make a difference with the future of the students

Although some in the media might not portray it, we know police officers do care about the people they serve!

How and Why People Change

Surely there are some things that you don't like about yourself. So you just decide to change them, right? Of course not: it isn't that simple. It's more likely that you will keep on doing those behaviors, even though you'd like to change them. Is that because the old saying "A leopard can't change his spots" is correct? No, I think people can change. Unfortunately, you can't just snap your fingers and say goodbye to deep-rooted patterns, even when those patterns result in bad consequences.

So, how do you change? From my experience, I believe we change our lives for three reasons. The first reason is you go through a life-cycle stage on a biological level, which turns you into a different person. Think about how a baby goes from crawling to walking to running. As humans, we are hard wired to make those developmental changes. As teenagers, our hormones command that we charge into adulthood, even if we aren't quite ready for the challenge! You go from puppy love to dating to marriage and perhaps even to raising a family of your own. At each stage you have a new opportunity to change and grow.

The second reason we change may come from the influence of an outside source: a trusted friend, a boss or an influential teacher who pushes you to adjust your behavior. Sometimes this push works, sometimes it doesn't. If the behavior modification is something you're open to and/or the change is required (i.e., you must stop smoking if you want to keep your job) then the odds are pretty good that you'll make the necessary change. Of course, when was the last time you were successful in causing another person to change through nagging or begging? The third and final reason that we'll change centers on pain. I'm talking about both psychological and physical agony—enough to cause you to want to relieve your discomfort. In these situations, it is no longer possible for you to keep living as you have been, and a change must be made. Let's take a look at a couple of theories on change and how they lead into motivational interviewing.

Self-Perception Theory

A person becomes more or less committed to an action based on the verbal stance they take on it. Once they begin talking about the benefits of change, they become more likely to make that change. An individual that defends his current behavior is less likely to change his behavior.

This can be summed up in one brief real-life example. For those of you who are married, have a boss or have ever had a boss, I know you've used this tactic at one time or another. It falls along the lines of, "Let's make him/her think it was their own idea."

But more seriously, this concept holds true with achieving goals. Think about a time when a younger officer tried to give you advice. When they told you what you should do. How did that go over? How did that make you feel? What if the advice was spot on? Did that still make you mad? As I said, it's very difficult to influence someone from the outside. Now consider how it would feel if you had already come up with the same idea on your own. How would that make you feel?

Here's a familiar scene; in fact I'm sure we've all come across this at one time or another. You're responding to a call, only to be greeted by an irate and furious person. Their level of fury is so

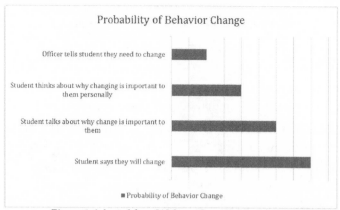

Figure 1 Adapted from Walters, Scott T. Motivating Offenders to Change a Guide for Probation and Parole. 2007.

extreme they can't even form complete words. Your inner voice smirks, "Try using your big boy words," while your reflexes get the better of you and you sternly say, "Calm down!" Kerosene meets fire, right? Now think about telling a college student that they shouldn't be drinking and even list a few valid reasons. They are underage, there are health risks, and safety risks, etc. I bet you know what happens next. The student digs his heels in and it becomes an argument. "But everyone else is doing it. You probably even drank when you were my age." Do you think this student is likely to move forward in the change process?

Prochaska's Stages of Change Theory

The stages of change theory is based on the concept that change occurs over a period of time, whereas behavior change traditionally was considered a one-time event, such as quitting drinking. After his father died of alcoholism, James Prochaska dedicated himself to finding a way to help people break their bad habits. As a psychologist at the University of Rhode Island, Prochaska spent years studying the responses of those who quit habits such as smoking, overeating and drinking on their own. During his investigations, he detected a pattern among those who were successful in changing their behavior. Amazingly, no matter the habit, these self-changers all progressed through the same stages along the way.

Prochaska's approach, referred to as the "stages of change" model, is simple but effective. Find your stage, and the model tells you what the next stage is and the strategies needed. Sometimes Prochaska's self-changers would regress and go back a stage or two, but once they returned to the strategies specific to their stage, they'd be right back on track.

> *"The only mistake you can make is to give up on yourself."* — James Prochaska

His model of change has 6 stages: pre-contemplation, contemplation, preparation, action, maintenance, and relapse. During the pre-contemplation stage, the students are not considering change or have decided the benefits of their current actions outweigh the negative. Contemplation is the stage where they think there may be a problem but as yet, they have not decided what to do about it. Preparation is where they take small steps and begin to plan. The action stage leads to actively making changes, which then leads to the maintenance stage. Following the action stage, many students will enter the last stage of relapse.[3] They will often learn something from the relapse and move through the stages faster the next time.

There are four main insights you can pull from the stages of change theory. The first is that change is in fact a process that occurs over time. Secondly, the stage at which a person finds him or herself will determine the approach needed to help them. With most interactions on campus, students will be in the very early stages, thus the goal of your

[3] Prochaska, James, and WF Velicer. "The Transtheoretical Model of Health Behavior Change." *The Science of Health Promotion* 12, no. 1 (1997): 38-48.

interaction is to prepare them for change. The third insight is that relapse is normal. For many people, it will be a process of trial and error before finally reaching success. Lastly, you may want to see the student progress through all of the stages, but I suggest it is a more realistic goal simply to raise their motivation to change.[4]

Working with the stages of change, you must meet the student at their current stage. The overall spirit of motivational interviewing is built around the client-centered style of interaction, but careful attention must be paid to the current stage of change. Looking into the stages, the strategies used at each stage vary. Earlier stages focus more on eliciting change talk and building confidence, whereas the later stages call for planning and support. If the officer does not meet the students where they are, it can have a reverse effect. It gives the students the impression they are being coerced, which in turn will undermine their own motivation to change making them less likely to change.

[4] Walters. *Motivating Offenders to Change.* 2007.

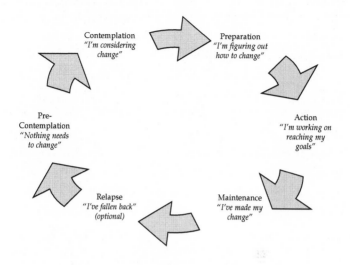

Contemplation
"I'm considering change"

Preparation
"I'm figuring out how to change"

Pre-Contemplation
"Nothing needs to change"

Action
"I'm working on reaching my goals"

Relapse
"I've fallen back"
(optional)

Maintenance
"I've made my change"

The Stages of Change

Let's revisit my student from the introduction. When we left him, I would say that he was in the pre-contemplation stage. He had already been caught a few times by both housing staff and the police. As I spoke with him, he began to move toward the contemplation stage and even danced on the edge of preparation.

He knew right away why we were there and appeared very nonchalant and unconcerned. This is likely due to the fact that he had been caught before and his life went on just fine.

Thus, there was no compelling reason in his mind to change. As I applied the OARS technique (I'll cover this in more detail in the next section), it flowed so naturally that the untrained eye would see it as just making small talk. Then almost as quickly as a seesaw switches when unbalanced, we began moving toward change talk. He began sharing his reasons for smoking cannabis: to deal with stress caused by school and being away from home, where his grandmother was ill. In my mind I saw a light bulb turn on. His internal motivation wasn't the negative health effects, the legal implications or sanctions at school. He told me that it was his grandmother.

From there, things were easy. A few OARS (mostly now reflections) and he pondered how his behavior wasn't helping his grandmother, i.e. frequent arrests, getting kicked out of school, etc. I didn't tell him these were the consequences, he came up with them on his own (see: why people change—this was HIS idea, wink, wink). This revelation that his behavior might be causing problems for his grandmother is the contemplation stage.

I then used a reflection on his caring for his grandmother and their close relationship. He naturally shared more about how important she is to him and that she is the one who raised him. I followed up with a summary of what he had just said about the consequences of not helping his grandmother. He agreed with my summary (no surprise, I just restated what he said).

I decided to push forward and dropped a call to action. "What could you do to help your grandmother?" I asked him, "What would that look like?" "What else?" He then created a verbal list of actions and steps he could take. Stop smoking, get the legal things cleared up so they weren't hanging over his head and go into the student standards office the next day to meet with them. He agreed that he could call his grandmother when he felt stressed instead of smoking. I then affirmed those steps, highlighting that those were very responsible steps to take and that they showed a great deal of character.

When I was done pointing out his character and responsible steps, the cop side of me came out; after a conversation like that it was easy. He came right out and told me about the cannabis he had, where it was in the room and then gave me consent to retrieve it.

Throughout that semester, I would occasionally see this student when I was on foot patrol. We knew each other by name and would stop to chat. I am happy to report that he is doing well and so is his grandmother.

Having an "enforcement" situation with an easy "confession" and handing over of contraband, helping a student move forward in the stages of change to stop smoking cannabis, creating a relationship that would lead to future community policing situations is a win/win/win. What more could a police officer ask for?

Imagine this scenario:
It's Monday and you are sitting in your pre-shift briefing when the lieutenant makes an announcement. The Chief has decided to implement a department-wide fitness program. What goes through your head?

If you're like me, a combination of thoughts:

- I don't need to work out. (Pre-contemplation)
- I guess I could be in better shape. Maybe this will be good for me. (Contemplation)
- How can I make this work? (Preparation)
- This will be easy; I already work out 5 days a week. (Action)
- I'm already in great shape; this will just let me maintain it at work! (Maintenance)
- Well, I was doing great about working out but have slacked off. This will help get me back on track. (Relapse)

Those, my friends, are what the stages of change sound like. Change doesn't happen overnight; it is a process.

As a freshman in college, I enjoyed the freedom from my parents and set out to explore this new-found world of independence. I fell into the "perceived social norm," that going out and drinking is a natural part of college and that everybody is doing it. At the start of my junior year, I found out I was heading to war. My eyes were wide open to the reality that I could die. So believe me when I say I lived it up while I could! When I survived and came back, guess what? I lived it up! After all, I had endured war and had experienced my share of near-death experiences. As graduation drew closer and I began to think about being in "the real world," I considered what my life after college would look like and where I wanted to be. Looking at the road I was on, I decided I wasn't on the right track. This is when I began thinking about change and then began preparing to change. This was tough for me, as the friends I hung out with were partiers and I was considered one, too. To try and break that reputation and those expectancies on my own was not easy. I did make some progress but would soon have short-term relapses, falling back into my old ways. This back and forth went on for some time.

As I entered graduate school, I had one class in particular that really gave me the tools to create a proper plan for behavior change. Dr. Thomas Hawkins (awesome man!) was my instructor and I don't think he saw how much he helped me change my life. Everything exponentially took off from there. I have since gone on and applied the same methods in order to change other behaviors, such as fitness, erasing bad habits and creating new, good habits of my choosing.

After personally walking this path and learning the ins and outs of how the stages of change work, I want in turn to help others. When I think back to that period of time when I was trying to make the changes I wanted to make without the proper tools, I realize what a long and tiresome road it was. If I can come alongside and shorten that walk for someone else, it would be a very rewarding experience.

Perhaps the most important thing you do in your job involves protection. As campus police, you're on the front lines of protecting the students from criminal activity, but your greatest service may come in the form of helping to protect these students from themselves. A great deal of care and focus goes into creating and maintaining a safe environment. Think of learning about and applying the techniques of motivational inter- viewing as another set of tools for you to use. Let's keep going and take a look at how motivational interviewing fits into college policing and your life.

SECTION III

We've looked at some of the different ways people learn and spent some time on the stages of change. Now let's hone in on motivational interviewing (MI). I was first introduced to MI in 2012. As the Crime Prevention Officer at EIU, one of my responsibilities was to co-teach some of the alcohol sanctioning classes. Dr. Heather Webb, Director of Student Standards, suggested I attend the "BASICS: Brief Assessment Screening and Intervention of College Students" two-day practitioner training.

During a training session, the instructor asked for a volunteer to play the role of a college freshman. I volunteered and joined him in front of the class, and we had an impromptu MI session. My role was to play a freshman in the pre-contemplative stage of change about drinking. While playing the part, I didn't just see how fluid the process of MI is, how it moves you through the stages of change; I also felt it. From this unique perspective, I was able to experience first-hand the gentle art of being quickly moved through change. I found it to be such a natural, effortless process that I would have had to work harder to NOT go with MI. From that moment on, I was all in.

Why College Students Drink

We've looked at how students learn and what motivates change. Now let's explore the different ways that MI is especially effective with college students. It's important to understand a few key themes: why students drink, the consequences of drinking and how campus police can be in the right place at the right time to make a difference.

From a student's perspective, there are some "positive" reasons to drink:

- Celebrating a special occasion ("I passed my mid-term exams!" "Our team won the national championship!")
- A drink or two may make it easier to express feelings or talk with members of the opposite sex. Liquid courage!
- Friends have a lot of influence, whether it is indirectly (someone hands you a beer when you walk into a party) or directly (expectations are that you will always party because you run with a crowd that parties)
- Thinking, "I am an adult and this is how adults socialize"
- Alcohol can relieve stress or bring some excitement to an otherwise boring routine

While there are some events where a lot of drinking is planned ahead of time ('We're getting hammered tonight!"), more frequently a student doesn't plan to overindulge. Instead he or she gets carried away (someone buys a round or everyone gets caught up in drinking games). In either case, if a person gets drunk by drinking five or more drinks in a couple of hours, this is considered high-risk drinking behavior. It has been reported that high-risk drinking affects almost 60% of college students at one time or another.[1]

In addition to the "positive" effects that students mistakenly convince themselves of, you don't have to look very far for a very powerful influence: it's on the television and movie screens. The way college drinking is portrayed on the big screen is very unrealistic. In fact, if you went by some of Hollywood's greatest hits, you'd think a party is filled with people either standing around having a great time or dancing to a hip band, nobody gets seriously injured in drunken brawls and if you do drink and drive, you usually end up unscathed or unharmed at the end of the night.

Our culture provides a blueprint for under-graduate alcohol abuse and comes close to show-casing it as a rite of passage. However, we all know that in the real world, the movies don't usually show what can happen when drinking

---

[1] "College Drinking." National Institute on Alcohol Abuse and Alcoholism. 2015. Accessed January 7, 2015.

gets out of hand...rape, assault, illness and more. Of course these scenes don't make it onto most movie screens because they are far from entertaining! Colleges may not be able to change how Hollywood portrays collegiate drinking, but the combination of campus police and MI can help increase the distance between Hollywood fantasy and real college life.

Campus police are on the front lines when it comes to dealing with students drinking. Whether strolling the quad or responding to a call, the subject of drinking comes up frequently. This helps, especially in the case of MI, because often these brief interactions (or interventions, if you will) are the only opportunity you will have. The luxury of a two-hour MI session in order to explore drinking habits is unrealistic.

Who Can Talk to College Students About Alcohol?

Almost all drinkers in college interact with people who are concerned about their health and safety, such as health-care workers, administrators, teachers, or resident assistants. In contrast, very few are referred to counselors who specialize in alcohol or drug abuse treatment. This means that more non-specialists will ultimately talk with a large number of college drinkers than specialized counselors will. Fortunately, there is good evidence that under certain circumstances, individuals with relatively little counseling training can impact college students' drinking.[2] "A caveat: although non-specialists can be effective in many contexts, there are times when a trained specialist such as a licensed counselor, social worker, or psychologist is the appropriate one to conduct an intervention. We believe that it is best to refer a student to such a person when the student is at risk for immediate alcohol related threats to safety, is suffering from mental health problems, abuse or has thoughts of suicide. These

---

[2] Quinn, Patrick D., and Kim Fromme. "Alcohol Use and Related Problems Among College Students and Their Noncollege Peers: The Competing Roles of Personality and Peer Influence*." *J. Stud. Alcohol Drugs Journal of Studies on Alcohol and Drugs,* 2011, 622-32.

sometimes serious problems should always be assessed and treated by a qualified professional."[3]

---

[3] Walters and Baer. *Talking with College Students About Alcohol*. 2006.

Campus Police

Overall, the role of campus police is a very dynamic one that involves wearing a lot of hats. It's not about just showing up and arresting the bad guys. In a typical day you can handle a wide range of complex issues including: mental disorders, medical emergencies, traffic violations, domestics, a wide gamut of drugs from pot to meth labs, lost puppies, flat tires, suicidal individuals and so on. College police are also educators who are teaching responsibility, accountability, campus safety and alcohol safety.

MI is a natural fit for this unique position on campus that allows you to educate and influence students. Your roles that make you ideally suited for MI include:

Being service oriented — No matter how you look at it, police are here to help and serve. You come to the rescue when someone is having a "not so good" day or you are enforcing the law to keep your community safe.

Problem solver — When people call the police it is because they have a problem they either don't know how to solve, can't solve alone or need help with. Sound familiar? You tailor the solution to the specific situation and person. You understand that there is rarely a set solution for every situation or individual. Police must take into account the totality of the circumstances and find an effective, efficient and workable solution to whatever the problem may be.

Skilled communicator — You must effectively communicate across language barriers, culturally diverse populations, emotionally-charged individuals, and people from all walks of life. The situation may be high-risk, making clear communication vital. This communication may include interviewing a witness, a suspect or even the victim of a crime. Consider the variety of communication skills needed. In your communication toolbox you can find words, tone, rate, body language and, don't forget, eye contact.

Accountability — This one seems simple enough: police hold others accountable for their actions.

Motivation experts — Your goals include cooperation and compliance. How do you achieve that? You find out what motivates a person in that given situation and discuss it with him or her in order to help the individual see the need to comply. Then you can help the person to see multiple perspectives and possible solutions and to weigh all the pros and cons. Throughout this encounter you are also guiding the student's thought process through emotional barriers.

As a campus police officer you are in the unique position to educate and influence those you come in contact with every day—both in formal and informal ways. You are here to serve and help. Adding MI to your repertoire will enhance your ability to motivate, problem solve and hold others accountable. Who doesn't need someone like that in their life?

How Motivational Interviewing Fits into Campus Policing

Officers are in a unique position to talk to students. First of all, officers in uniform possess a certain level of authority or "position of power" when talking to someone just by being in uniform. Secondly, when faced with a possible enforcement situation (i.e. an underage student found in possession of alcohol), that student's motivation to change is very high. Before that contact with the officer, the student likely was not thinking about his drinking behavior or whether he should change that behavior. There's something about coming in contact with an officer that will often trigger thoughts about a change in behavior. Funny how that works!

Imagine being pulled over for speeding. Regardless of whether you get a ticket or not, you will spend the next few minutes or days paying more attention to your speed. These change thoughts are triggered without any evoking or talking. You are prompted by an interaction with a person in uniform.

As a campus police officer, what better time to talk about change and strengthen that motivation to change. Rather than start at a lower level and work to strengthen a student's motivation to change, start strengthening that motivation when it is at a higher point. Starting the change process closer to the incident is key. Often students get drinking tickets, DUIs or minor possession tickets and a large amount of time goes by before they begin the sanctioning process. Court dates are usually scheduled 30 days out. In court a student might then be assigned to the next scheduled alcohol treatment program. More than a month can slip away before anyone begins to initiate the change process. If students are referred to the student conduct office, then it will be a few weeks before they enter an alcohol sanctioning class.

This time gap allows for life to go on for the students. They have moved on and resumed their lives. They then enter the programs with a lower motivation level regarding their drinking behavior. They might even be lower than before they "got caught," as they have seen the drinking ticket wasn't "the end of the world."

The magic is bringing MI to the first contact when motivation for change is naturally higher. This allows a natural flow into starting the change processes before "life goes on." When they enter the sanctioning process, the student will have already begun the change process and will ideally move through the processes farther.

After I met with our pot smoker and walked him through MI, the next step was his meeting with the student standards office to discuss the incident. This was done so that the school could get his side of the story and then from there, the staff members were able to determine the best route for sanctioning. What's important to point out is that this entire process — in the field from me as a cop, to the student standards process and during the sanctioning phase — adhered to the principles of MI. The student was continually met where he was in the MI process.

> *MI provides a jump-start towards change.*

Different Settings for Motivational Interviewing

Motivational interviewing has years of research and evidence to show that it is a great way to help people with their alcohol or substance abuse problems. As we will cover later in this section, MI is now being successfully used in 9 other areas. Policing is a very dynamic role, and every situation is different from the last. Motivational interviewing is an excellent fit for police officers as it complements your strengths. We will explore different settings where you can apply MI, but I challenge you to bring this proven method to other areas and situations as you patrol the campus.

Enforcement

Just a reminder that just like any police work, using common sense about when to apply the techniques of MI is key. MI isn't meant for highly intoxicated people. For some reason people always ask me, "Well aren't they going to be too drunk for it to work?" Of course if someone is at the level of intoxication at which they can't walk or form complete sentences then it is safe to say that MI will be less effective! Pay attention to the red flags that come up and use those police instincts you've honed to let you know when the time is appropriate. You will become very frustrated if you try MI on every single person you come across, especially if they are over-served. It's important to understand that part of what makes MI work is that you are meeting the people where they are. If they're too inebriated they will not be able to understand the nuances of the process. You can always try again another time. The chances are good that in the near future you will come across these people in a similar situation again. Hopefully, they won't be as drunk.

There was one night when I responded to a report of an intoxicated individual in a residence hall bathroom. Throwing up! Oh joy, we all love these calls! Clearly MI wouldn't work as the student needed medical attention and was too out of it to engage in conversation. The student went to the ER and life went on.

Fast forward to a week later, and guess whose room we visited in response to a loud party complaint? Bingo! Our student who had been too intoxicated the week before was now just listening to loud music, which gave me a perfect opportunity to engage in some MI.

There were two roommates and they had only begun to drink, so they were not highly intoxicated. Keeping in mind that there was a "negative consequence" from just a week ago as we went through the MI process, the student began to really reflect on that night and explored her feelings about blacking out, going to the ER and what that all really meant. She also now had two "run-ins" with campus police.

Research shows that students report being arrested or receiving a citation as the most perceived negative consequence from drinking.

Community Policing

On a college campus, you can easily find opportunities to talk about drinking even when you least expect it. I clearly remember a time when I was working at one of our football games. I was tasked with overseeing one of the gates. I worked alongside some students, who were in charge of collecting the tickets as people entered the gates. After the game began, things really slowed down, so small talk and a casual conversation began. There was one male (big and tall guy) and one female (track athlete) working the entrance. The guy joked that his friends gave him the nickname "Giraffe" because when he gets drunk, he is very wobbly and has a hard time walking. Boom! He had brought up high-risk drinking, so I thought, "Why not MI?" He initially shared the story thinking it was funny and cool (I really think he was just trying to impress the girl).

I went into a casual MI mode with him and just as with our pot smoker, he began to see things in a different light. Another interesting thing about that conversation was that these two students, who didn't really know each other, began to meaningfully interact. We were all engaged in a REAL and intellectual conversation! It turned out to be a great way to pass the time and was much cooler than small talk. The added bonus is that it may have had some lasting effects. There are other times that I've had the opportunity to casually bring up high risk drinking while walking through the lobbies of the residence halls in the evenings. When I stop to have a friendly conversation with the students, it is easy to ask about the other students in the building. Usually my conversation sounds something along the lines of, "We don't have many complaints out of this res hall. Are there many partiers at all here?" or "When you guys hang out in the lobby, do you get a kick out of the silly drunk kids passing by?" I take an indirect approach to bringing up drinking rather than asking them about their own drinking. I never want to assume they are drinkers or have high-risk drinking tendencies, but if they are, it is an easy transition to MI. By having these conversations on a casual basis, it builds rapport and sets the tone for a spontaneous conversation about drinking.

Sanctioning

While serving as the crime prevention officer, I had the opportunity to practice and develop my MI skills while co-teaching the alcohol sanction classes with the assistant director of student standards. Our approach to these classes was to create a comfortable, non-confrontational environment in which the students felt comfortable discussing the good and not so good things related to high-risk drinking. We would share educational information about alcohol, and when the students requested it, we would provide advice. We were merely facilitators helping to set the environment and guide the conversations. The students would share the reasons to change and would work together to come up with different ways to make those changes. After all, they are the experts on themselves, not me!

This was a very enjoyable interaction with students that accomplished a variety of things. The students voiced the reasons to change, developed plans to change and even helped to clarify the perceived norms and actual drinking norms. A bonus: in a majority of the class evaluations the students reported their attitudes, perceptions and understanding of the police departments were far more positive than they were before the class. Just like the old saying—"two birds with one stone." You can help students change their high-risk drinking behavior and change the image of the police department all in one swoop!

Who Currently Uses Motivational Interviewing?

MI was first developed for the field of addiction, but it has broadened in scope and has become a popular method in a variety of settings. Here are a few of the ways it is commonly used:

College alcohol education programs: Many colleges and universities use MI in alcohol intervention courses for on-campus violations or sanctions — this can include one-on-one sessions, group classes that last from one to four hours or extended programs that span a longer period of time (days or weeks).

Health practitioners: Weight loss management, encouraging healthy eating and treating diabetes are just some of the ways that practitioners use MI in their daily interactions with patients.

Corrections officers: It has been introduced to the criminal justice system in general and probation efforts specifically — it is used to build skills in compliance and for increasing an offender's readiness for behavior change. A person gets MI in jail, then when they are on probation, and then again when they are in a treatment program after probation. The key is consistency!

Substance abuse (addiction services): MI is used to show the difference between a client's unhealthy behaviors (such as binge drinking, smoking, doing drugs) and their own healthy goals (their desire to do well in school, be responsible and be a good person) in the hope that focusing on the difference will motivate the client to change.

Mental health: MI helps doctors and patients develop strong, collaborative relationships in order to reduce resistance to change.

Psychiatry: MI is used in a variety of psychiatric settings such as anger management, depression and other mental health programs.

Primary health-care: MI is client-centered; it is goal-driven and directional. That makes it a good fit when a clear, positive behavioral change is required, such as losing weight, taking medication, etc.

Tobacco cessation and recovery: Motivational interviewing can be used in counseling tobacco-dependent clients. The goal is to help clients move toward being ready to change behavior, NOT to get someone to quit using tobacco.

Vocational rehabilitation: Motivation is an important element in returning to work. Initial studies using MI in the employment field are encouraging. It is used as a technique to allow practitioners to involve clients in resolving their ambivalence about work and employment opportunities.

With the wide range of areas in which MI can be used successfully, it's important to recognize that you can turn your everyday work routine into an ongoing learning laboratory! You can evolve and develop your skills in almost any environment. Remember the essential ingredient: put your trust in the MI process. Know that with experience, you will develop greater insight and faith in your ability to participate in the "dance" that occurs with complex and productive interpersonal communication. In the next section, we will look at some of the specific hurdles you will encounter using MI as a campus police officer and how you can deal with these issues.

Origin of Motivational Interviewing

Motivational interviewing first began when American psychologist William R. Miller spent three months at the Hjellestad Clinic in Norway in 1982. During this time, he met a group of psychologists who were interested in discussing how he would respond to difficult situations they had encountered when treating people with alcohol problems. "As I explained and demonstrated how I counseled alcoholics, they asked wonderful probing questions about why I said what I did, what I was thinking, and why I pursued one line and not another,"[4] Miller would later explain. "They coaxed from me a specification of what I was doing and why. I wrote this down in a somewhat long and rambling manuscript, which I shared with a few colleagues."[4] One of these colleagues was Dr. Ray Hodgson, then editor for Behavioral Psychotherapy Journal. Miller's manuscript, "Motivational interviewing with problem drinkers," was published in the British Journal of Behavioral Psychotherapy in 1983. In the article, Miller described MI as a "common sense, pragmatic

---

[4] Bein, Thomas H., William R. Miller, and Joseph M. Boroughs. "Motivational Interviewing with Alcohol Outpatients." Behav. Psychother. Behavioural Psychotherapy, 1993.

approach based on principles derived from effective counseling practice and experience." He said that motivation was not a personality trait but was part of the process of change in which contemplation and preparation are important early steps that can be influenced by the counselor.[5]

Miller's article generated a lot of interest from the research world. In 1989, Miller was on a sabbatical at the National Drug and Alcohol Research Centre in Sydney, Australia, when he met the British psychologist Stephen Rollnick. He prompted Miller to become more serious about describing and explaining elements of MI in greater detail. The two of them collaborated on the first book, Motivational Interviewing: Preparing People to Change Addictive Behavior, which was published in 1991.[6]

So you may be asking yourself: what is MI these days? It is a collaborative conversation style for strengthening a person's own motivation and commitment to change. It is a conversation about

---

[5] Miller, William R., and Stephen Rollnick. Motivational Interviewing: Helping People Change. 3rd ed. New York, NY: Guilford Press, 2013.

[6] "Ibid"

---

change and a method for helping people explore and resolve ambivalence. Let's break it down:

- Client-centered — Each person has an innate capacity and responsibility for making choices in how to behave.

- Directive — The counselor picks certain statements or questions that steer the conversation in a particular direction.

- Ambivalence — Most drinkers have mixed feelings about alcohol.

The Motivational Interviewing Style

MI is not a simple five-step sequence of questions for promoting change. Doing MI the right way involves a lot more than just asking questions — it demands active listening and affirming. Just as with any police enforcement situation, the style you use in your interaction can greatly affect the outcome. As you know from experience, officers become very skilled at tailoring their style to suit the interaction.

For many decades, police departments across the U.S. have used 10-codes as verbal shorthand when calling in incidents. This can be heard in radio communication, as police officers speak in a short, clear, and concise manner so they don't take up a lot of air-time. You only use this style in casual conversation with fellow officers, but not when talking to "civilians."

Or you may find yourself conducting a high-risk traffic stop (i.e., the person is suspected to be armed and dangerous). As you take cover from behind your squad car, you tap into your "cop voice," which is loud, commanding and authoritative. You shout out clear and concise directions: "Turn off the engine." "Throw your keys out the window." The message is simple and to the point. Your tone reflects that you are in charge and the listener must submit to your authority.

On the other end of the spectrum, in the course of a day, you may find yourself sitting down to interview a victim of sexual assault. Sexual assaults are one of the most traumatic types of criminal victimization. The victims find it difficult to discuss their victimization and even worse, they find it painful. You approach these interviews with the utmost empathy, respect and patience. Given the sensitivity of the situation, you are careful in choosing the location of the interview, the background noise, the people around you, the victim's seat in relation to the officer's seat, tone and rate of speech. Thought will be given to how you frame your questions, to your body posture and how you proceed.

These are just a few examples of how you are already tailoring your interactions to fit the situation without even realizing it. MI is just a natural extension of what you already do every day.

> *"Qualities of the provider, the student, and the interaction between them all influence change (or lack thereof) in the students behavior."*[7]

The overall style of MI is one of encouragement and guidance. Ambivalence is a normal stage of preparing for change, and this is where students can remain stuck for a long time. If you use a direct, confrontational style it is more likely to bring out an argumentative response from the individual. However, if you use the MI style, you'll find that a person will more likely be persuaded by what they hear themselves say.

Let's take a moment to revisit our friend from the first chapter. When we first met up with him, the student had been previously caught but still continued to smoke. He didn't see any need for changing his behavior and was not thinking about change. If I had come right out and presented him with options, information and advice for changing his behavior (preparation stage) or even offered planning assistance (action stage), things would not have gone so smoothly. He began in the pre-contemplation stage and as I talked to him he moved to contemplation and even flirted with the

---

[7] Walters and Baer. *Talking with College Students About Alcohol*. 2006.

preparation stage. The student standards office (whose staffers are also trained in MI) met him in the contemplation stage and continued strengthening his motivation as he moved through the stages of change.

When you don't meet the students where they are in the stages of change and instead expect them to meet you, the students will feel the need to defend the status quo. They will dig in their heels and defend their reasons against change. This in turn will only reinforce their current behavior. It's very important to meet people where they are at that point.

There are four fundamental principles that apply to the processes of motivational interviewing:

Principle 1: Express Empathy

Empathy helps you understand the issues from the student's point of view. When a student feels that he is understood, he is more likely to open up to his own experiences and share with you (or others). Individuals become more comfortable fully examining their ambivalence about change and are less likely to become defensive. Having them share their experiences with you in depth allows you to assess when and where they need support and what potential pitfalls may need to be focused on in the change planning process. Goal: building rapport enables change.

Principle 2: Develop Discrepancy

"Motivation for change occurs when people perceive a discrepancy between where they are and where they want to be."[8]   When people understand that their current behavior doesn't align with their future goals, they become more motivated to change. The best way to do this is to gradually and gently persuade them that some of their current ways of doing things may take them further from rather than toward their goals. Goal: talk about pros and cons.

Principle 3: Roll with Resistance

In MI, you don't fight resistance; you "roll with it." You help a person develop their own solutions to the problems they define. When you come up against a concern, don't impose a new way of thinking; encourage exploring problems with a different perspective. This will cut down on

---

[8] Miller, William R. *Motivational Enhancement Therapy Manual: A Clinical Research Guide for Therapists Treating Individuals with Alcohol Abuse and Dependence*. Rockville, Md. (6000 Executive Blvd., Rockville 20892-7003): U.S. Dept. of Health and Human Services, Public Health Service, National Institutes of Health, National Institute on Alcohol Abuse and Alcoholism, 1995.

arguments and defensive behavior. Goal: respect the student's independence.

Principle 4: Support Self-Efficacy

A person's belief that he can change is a huge motivator to succeeding in making a change. Remind those going through the process of change that there is no right way to change — you are only limited by your own imagination! Focus on successful changes that have been made in the past in order to show that change is possible. Goal: help the individuals understand that they are capable of change.

Evidence-Based Results

For the purposes of offering some evidence-based results, I am including the results of three different studies done over the years. These results are by no means definitive and are provided to show that the findings are encouraging: MI is an effective treatment. In most cases, MI is more effective than no treatment at all and is at least as effective as other viable treatments for a wide variety of problems, including alcohol and substance abuse.

From Rediscovering Fire: Small Interventions, Large Effects

William R. Miller's study at the University of New Mexico: The Drinker's Check-Up (DCU) was developed as an intervention for initial tests of the efficacy of motivational interviewing. Within a generally empathic and supportive style, the DCU provides personal feedback of findings from an assessment of drinking and related problems. To enhance discrepancy, the individual's scores are compared with population norms, a form of feedback found to induce modest behavior change even when provided by mail.[9]   The therapist

---

[9] Agostinelli, Gina, Janice M. Brown, and William R. Miller. "Effects of Normative Feedback on Consumption among Heavy Drinking College Students." *Journal of Drug Education*, 1995, 31-40.

solicited the client's own reactions to feedback. They elicited and reflected the client's personal concerns, perceptions of drinking and related problems. They were also able to elicit the client's personal reasons for change. In a first controlled trial, self-referred problem drinkers given a DCU showed significant reductions in drinking within 6 weeks.[10] When the waiting list group was subsequently assessed and given a DCU, a comparable reduction in drinking was observed. Similar findings emerged in a second trial, with 69% reduction in drinking in the DCU condition. Problem drinkers assigned to a waiting list showed no apparent reduction during the same period but a 58% reduction after a subsequent DCU.[11]

According to the **Blueprint for Implementing Evidence-Based Alcohol Prevention Policy and Programs in the Collegiate Environment**:

Screening and motivational interviewing was tested in the college setting at the University of

---

[10] Miller, William R., R. Gayle Sovereign, and Barbara Krege. "Motivational Interviewing with Problem Drinkers: II. The Drinker's Check-up as a Preventive Intervention." *Behav. Psychother. Behavioural Psychotherapy*, 1988, 251.

[11] Bein, Thomas H., William R. Miller, and Joseph M. Boroughs. "Motivational Interviewing with Alcohol Outpatients." *Behav. Psychother. Behavioural Psychotherapy,* 1993, 347.

Washington. This program involves screening students for their behavior as it relates to alcohol use and abuse. Those students who are heavy drinkers, as defined by the scored screening instrument, are then involved in a one-on-one meeting with a university representative. The meeting with high-risk drinkers involves a non-confrontational approach. Follow-up motivational interviews discuss life planning and how alcohol fits into life plans.

Assessment of screening and motivational interviewing conducted over a four-year period at the University of Washington found that individuals who engaged in motivational interviewing after screening drank less than similar students who did not engage in motivational interviewing.

According to **Effects of Motivational Interviewing Intervention on Blackouts Among College Freshmen**:

Conclusions: MI had an impact on reducing alcohol consumption and the rate of blackouts among college freshmen who were engaging in high-risk drinking and illicit drug use.

Clinical Relevance: The findings support the importance of using MI with freshmen college students to decrease drinking and the associated negative consequences, including blackouts. This finding has particular relevance for registered nurses, physicians, and community health nurses. One goal was to reduce alcohol consumption and its negative consequences for students. The program was modeled after the MI harm-reduction/alcohol skills-training approach. Participants received MI at baseline and again at 2 weeks, 3 months, and 6 months. Assessments were completed at baseline and again at 6 months. The MI program was delivered in two brief 50-minute therapy sessions — one following the baseline assessment, and one at the 2-week visit. The booster sessions were 50 minutes in length and were held at 3 months and 6 months after the 2-week visit. Participants met individually with trained peer interventionists, who delivered the MI program incorporating alcohol education and personalized feedback.[12]

At baseline, the interventionists oriented the students to the MI program. They built rapport; assessed drinking history and behavior (i.e., consumption, consequences, beliefs, and readiness to change); and encouraged a commitment to participate. Students completed questionnaires to

[12] Dimeff, Linda A. *Brief Alcohol Screening and Intervention for College Students (BASICS): A Harm Reduction Approach.* New York: Guilford Press, 1999.

assist in the assessment of their alcohol use and its negative consequences.

The aim of this study was to examine the impact of an MI program on the rate of the participants' blackouts between baseline and 6 months. The results showed a significant decrease in the weekly number of drinks, weekly number of hours drinking and drinking days. In addition, the frequency of drug use decreased from 27.1% at baseline to 23.4% at 6 months. These findings are consistent with prior research demonstrating that an MI intervention has an impact on drinking and drug use.[13],[14],[15] These findings suggest that the MI program had an impact on the participants' alcohol consumption as well as their rate of blackouts.

[13] Branscum, Paul, and Manoj Sharma. "A Review of Motivational Interviewing-Based Interventions Targeting Problematic Drinking Among College Students." *Alcoholism Treatment Quarterly,* 2010, 63-77.

[14] D'amico, Elizabeth J., Karen Chan Osilla, and Sarah B. Hunter. "Developing a Group Motivational Interviewing Intervention for First-Time Adolescent Offenders At-Risk for an Alcohol or Drug Use Disorder." *Alcoholism Treatment Quarterly*, 2008, 417-36.

[15] Fernandes, Simone, Maristela Ferigolo, Mariana Canellas Benchaya, Taís De Campos Moreira, Pollianna Sangalli Pierozan, Cláudia Galvão Mazoni, and Helena Maria Tannhauser Barros. "Brief Motivational Intervention and Telemedicine: A New Perspective of Treatment to Marijuana Users." *Addictive Behaviors,* 2010, 750-55.

The findings from the studies suggest that MI is a promising tool that can effectively help students. Now let's dive in and learn the various MI techniques in the next chapter.

SECTION IV

How to Use Motivational Interviewing

Motivation is defined as the reason or reasons one has for behaving in a certain way. Personal desire to do something. This is an important concept because in every aspect of life, there are situations in which you may want to motivate yourself or others to do something. Motivation is always changing and shifting—it can grow, decrease or even change focus. It can come in two different forms: extrinsic or intrinsic. Extrinsic motivation comes from outside influences: earning a paycheck (a reward or prize) or paying fines (fear of punishment) in order to create a change. Intrinsic motivation is found within: the desire to change comes because a person wants to accomplish a goal or complete a task because it is something he or she enjoys doing. In the long run, internally motivated change has much longer lasting effects than does externally motivated change.

Motivational interviewing taps into the internal factor and relies on the belief that people are motivated to change their behavior when they become aware of the difference between where they currently are and where they want to be. Highlighting this discrepancy is done through an interactive process and is behavior specific. The idea is to get people to identify their own discrepancies and desires to change rather than have you tell them what to do. Let's take a closer look at MI in action.

How Motivational Interviewing Works

Motivational interviewing starts with a collaborative and friendly approach. It is important that you have empathy toward the person you're dealing with and that you recognize that a resistance to change, however much it's needed, is typical. We'll discuss this in more detail in the next section, but the bottom line is you can't take it personally when someone struggles! In fact, the best outcomes are when you are able to let go and allow the other person to be responsible for his or her own progress. You're there to support and affirm the student.

The objective is not to solve the problem or even to develop a plan; the goal is to help the person resolve his or her ambivalence, develop some momentum and believe that behavior change is possible. I know it's tempting with time constraints and other limitations (what if you don't see this person again?) to jump in and offer quick solutions. As a police officer, you're used to handling problems quickly and efficiently, but this is different. In fact, the more you interfere, the chances are high that you may deny the person the opportunity to explore his own problems. Allowing him to consider all of the issues ahead of him through the MI techniques will increase the chances that he will find an acceptable resolution. And you will have played a part in that process — win-win!

The Spirit of Motivational Interviewing

Before we get into the techniques and strategies of MI, I want to point out the importance of working with the spirit of motivational interviewing. As this process is fluid, it's key to meet the people where they are and to move them along, keeping a few principles in mind:

- Motivation to change must come from the person and cannot be imposed by you from the outside.

- It is the student's responsibility to resolve any ambivalence.

- The style of interaction is typically quiet; you're focused on getting the person to share his or her thoughts.

- Your goal is to help the student to examine and resolve ambivalence.

- Your interpersonal interaction plays a part in the student's readiness to change.

- This process is more like a partnership or collaboration rather than an expert vs. novice.

With MI, it is useful to have in mind an overall format for a session. In general, think of a session moving through four fundamental processes:

Engaging: Your goal is to create a collaborative working relationship with the student. You will work to make the student feel comfortable and like an active participant in the conversation. During the engaging process, you should focus on building rapport, trust and mutual respect.

Focusing: This is the part of the process where you guide students in an effort to clarify the picture of where they are headed. You may use this step to focus on specific steps they can take to get where they want to be. During focusing, you need to find the balance between actively directing the student and allowing the student to lead the conversation.

Evoking: You will work to bring to mind students' values and goals; help them recall past experiences that have been successful and reflect on what is working well in their lives. Open-ended questions will help evoke what is important to the students, which will then evolve into the planning phase.

Planning: This is the final step of the process, where the student begins change talk and you can guide him or her to form a plan of action. People are much more likely to follow through with a plan that they've said aloud and shared with someone else.

While these steps are somewhat linear, it's important to stress that MI is a fluid process. You will not necessarily go through each stage progressively; in fact, during a successful change conversation, I have often found myself circling back in order to move forward.

There is a basic approach to MI, and you shouldn't be surprised to learn that it involves the acronym we brought up earlier: OARS.[1]

OARS stands for:

    Open-ended questions

    Affirmations

    Reflections

    Summarizing

The image of OARS is a good one—just like moving along the water in a boat with paddles, MI is not about moving quickly. This isn't a speedboat that is powering from one place to another. It's not

---

[1] Miller, William R., and Stephen Rollnick. Motivational Interviewing: Helping People Change. 3rd ed. New York, NY: Guilford Press, 2013.

a sailboat either, completely dependent on the wind for movement. OARS gives you the ability to get the boat going in the right direction and with some sustained effort, can take you (and the student) a long way.

Putting Motivational Interviewing into Practice

So, you're ready to get started! While the concept of motivational interviewing sounds great on paper, the thought of practicing it with a student can be overwhelming. I had the advantage of attending two different training workshops on MI when I was working at the EIU Police Department. I then brought the same approach I used while working those overnight shifts at the sheriff's office—Read/Learn/Practice. My recommendation is to gain some experience by role-playing with other officers, staff or even family members.

Once you feel you're ready to involve students, start small with just one question, such as, "What are you looking for from your time here at the university?" This is where OARS kicks in. You begin with an open-ended and non-confrontational question, which is good at getting the conversation started. You will be surprised by the ideas people come up with when given the opportunity!

I also want to emphasize that MI is less about the specific words or strategies that you use and more about the spirit you bring to the conversation. Don't be afraid of saying the wrong thing. After you have a few experiences under your belt, your approach will become more natural to you. With MI, you will always receive instant feedback! If the student is responding in an open conversation and you are moving forward with your questions, then you are doing it right. An individual's responses will let you know where you stand. When you are first starting out, it can be easier to have a script to work from.

Techniques and Strategies

OARS

Now that you're ready to get into the meat of MI, let's take a closer look at OARS. As you've seen in the previous section, open-ended questions are those that can't be answered with a simple yes or no. An open-ended question allows an individual to create a forward momentum that you can use in helping them explore change. Let's go back to that night when I was called to the student's res hall room to investigate the smell of pot. I began the conversation with an open-ended question: "What difficulties have you had with smoking pot? How has it gotten you in trouble?"

This allowed him to express his own thoughts and the conversation then followed from his perspective. If I had simply said, "Have you experienced negative consequences from smoking?" he could have shut the conversation down with a simple "no." From the cop side, this question provides insight into whether there has been any criminal activity without having to directly ask, "Have you been arrested or in trouble for this before?" Nothing better than killing two birds with one stone!

Open-ended questions help you understand the other person's point of view and encourage the person to share their feelings about the situation; questions facilitate dialogue.

Here are some samples of open-ended questions:

Who is the most important person in your life?

Why are they important to you?

What was the best five minutes of your day?

When are you most likely to drink/do drugs/____?

How does your behavior affect those who are important to you?

What do you know about the risks of drinking/drugs?

What do you want to do next?

Affirmations are statements of recognition about someone's strengths. Many students who are open to MI are failed self-changers. That is, they've tried to alter their behavior on their own without success. Having been one of those folks myself, I know it left me in a place where I was suspicious that change was even possible. So by taking that empathy and knowledge from my own experience, I am able to apply it to MI. The first step is often affirming that change is possible and that they are capable of achieving change. For example, after the student told me that he had tried to quit smoking before, I said, "You were able to stop smoking for a week. How were you able to do that?" As I listened to his response, I was able to affirm those positive qualities he listed and point out his strengths and aspirations. I said, "Those strengths can help you quit smoking."

Affirming and supporting can go a long way in building rapport. When you consider that a student may be struggling with alcohol or drugs, it's not hard to imagine that affirmations are not something they're used to hearing! I want to point out that this support must be genuine — if someone believes that you are being insincere then rapport can be destroyed rather than built. Once I knew the student's internal motivation was his grandmother, I affirmed the fact that he cared and worried about her. I was able to affirm that he really just wanted to help her but wasn't sure how. As a cop, you already use a wide variety of these affirmations in order to build rapport. With MI, your focus changes a bit, to hone in on behavior change. You are taking skills you already utilize and shifting them towards the focus for positive change.

Here are a few examples of affirming responses:

I appreciate that you are willing to talk with me today.

You are clearly a very thoughtful person.

You handled yourself really well in that situation.

I've enjoyed talking with you today.

You are very courageous to be so revealing about this.

You really care about your health. (Future, education...)

When affirming is done right, it supports self-efficacy and promotes the idea that change is possible. Affirmations can strengthen motivation, confidence and rapport.

Reflections are the key to making MI work. The best motivational advice I can give you is to listen carefully — whenever you are in doubt about what to do, listen. But remember that this is a directive approach — you will actively guide the student forward. You will focus on change talk and shift the conversation if there is non-change talk. For example, "You are not quite sure you are ready to make a change, but you are aware that your drug use has caused concerns in your relationships, affected your school work and that it doesn't help your grandmother." When you are reflecting, make sure you vary the types of reflections so that you don't always just stay on the surface.

There are generally three different levels of reflective listening:

- **Repeating/rephrasing**: you repeat or rephrase what the speaker has said, staying close to the original statements

- **Paraphrasing:** you create a new statement in which the speaker's intention is implied

- **Reflection of feeling:** you emphasize the emotional aspects of the conversation

On each of these levels, you can modify the degree of reflection. If you are able to offer reflections that have some intensity, they can be powerful motivators. For example, when I said to the student, "Your grandmother's health has you worried; it seems very painful for you," it shifted the emotional tone and moved our conversation to a deeper level. If I had been wrong or if the student hadn't been ready to talk about it, he would have corrected me and the conversation still would have moved forward. This is the fluid part of MI—you always want to create forward motion and then harness that momentum in order to create change.

A good rule of thumb when using reflections is to use three reflections for every one question asked. Too many questions can cause an abrupt shift in the momentum and can even stop a conversation in its tracks. It can make even a simple conversation feel like an interrogation under bright lights, straight out a movie. Even though there are times you will want to create a shift or pause, for the most part you will want to keep the conversation flowing. Just as with all aspects of MI, reflections are a collaboration between you and the other person. You want to mirror what the student is saying in a non-threatening and non-judgmental manner so that you can help them understand themselves better. Use language that they are familiar with and avoid making generalizations or overstatements. Using some common phrases may help you while you are practicing reflections until the skill becomes second nature.

Here are some common reflection phrases:

> *So you feel...*
>
> *It sounds like you...*
>
> *You're wondering if...*
>
> *This is what I am hearing. Please correct me if I am wrong...*

To sum up: reflections are your way to check in with the student to ensure you know what's going on, rather than assuming you understand what they mean, and take the conversation to a deeper level.

Summarizing is a way to build on the reflections — summaries are an effective way to communicate your interest in a person, call attention to the key part of the conversation and shift direction, if necessary. As you get more comfortable with summarizing, you'll find a rhythm that works for you. I find that offering summaries often, especially at first, is a good way to keep the conversation on point. The basic structure of each summary starts with an announcement that you are about to summarize and then a list of what you have heard. You should offer an invitation for the other person to correct any information you may have misunderstood. Here's an example of my conversation: "Let me stop and sum up what we've just talked about. You're dealing with a lot of stress and worrying about your grandmother's health. You've had some thoughts about what's been happening, including how much you've been using and how it has affected your life, especially your health and your grades. Did I miss anything? I'm wondering what you think about these things."

The tricky part with summarizing is to not to let your inner police take over — you're not gathering evidence here, you're simply reflecting what the student has said in order for them to supply the meaning. Be careful to focus on the student's understanding of the problem and not let your wisdom or experience keep you from listening to their understanding of the situation. Miller and Rollnick refer to this as the "righting reflex." It's human nature to get caught up in a heart-felt argument for change, but that will not help the student. If you find yourself taking up the cause, mentally step back and shift your focus from direct persuasion to focusing on the student's interpretation of the circumstances. Just to be clear: avoid the righting reflex!

> Here are some samples of summary statements:
>
> *Let me see if I understand so far...*
>
> *Here is what I've heard. Tell me if I've missed anything.*
>
> *Did I hear you correctly?*
>
> *We covered that well. Now let's talk about...*

Summarizing will help the student understand the problem more clearly, and it is from this understanding that you can guide the student to consider change.

Change Talk

DARN-CAT

The goal of using OARS is to move the person forward by eliciting change talk, or self-motivational statements. Change talk refers to the student's discussion of his or her Desire, Ability, Reason, and Need to change behavior along with a Commitment to changing. You know how when you are able to talk out a problem, sometimes finding the solution yourself is more powerful than when someone else makes the suggestion? Change talk is a signal that the person is leaning in the direction of change. It may sound simple, but if you're not tuned in, you may miss it. The acronym DARN helps you recognize change talk when you hear it.

Desire:

> I want to get better grades.
>
> I wish I were more comfortable going out and not drinking.
>
> I would like to cut back on my drinking.

Ability:

> I could probably cut back on drinking.

> I can drink water instead of beer.

> I might be able to limit my number of drinks.

Reason:

> I know I would feel better if I didn't take shots.

> I might get better sleep at night.

> I want to stay in school.

Need:

> I need to not drink as much.

> I have to start going to my 8 am class.

> I have to get better grades.

The student has now voiced his reasons and motivation for change, but how do you turn that motivation into action? This is explained through another acronym: CAT. Commitment, Activation and Taking Steps. Commitment language indicates the likelihood of action. A person can say they "want to" or "wish" as many times as they want, but it is the actions that we are aiming for. Compare this to a contract declaring what will be done. The second is activation language, which indicates movement toward action and implies a commitment without directly stating it. Activation language is not as strong as commitment language. The third being taking steps; that is when a student states something they have already done in the direction of change. If the student had a previous run-in with the police, he or she may have already made some behavior changes. All of these types of commitment language are great targets for affirmations.

Commitment:

> I will limit my number of drinks.

> I could say no to taking shots.

> I am going to only go out on weekends.

Activation

> I am willing to limit my number of nights out.

> I am prepared to not take shots anymore.

> I am ready to make a change.

Taking Steps

> I didn't go out during the week this week.

> I said no to taking shots last night.

> I made sure to walk home instead of driving.

A few ways to use OARS and elicit change talk are to ask about present concerns, such as the downsides of drinking. Questions asking about the past or about the future are very powerful in bringing out change talk. They would sound something like, "Tell me about the last time you got really drunk. What happened?" Or "How will your drinking change in the long run?" Toward the end of an MI interaction, it can be helpful to ask, "Where does this leave you in terms of your drinking?" Asking directly about change will likely elicit change talk and bring you to the brink of commitment.

A large part of the process of motivational interviewing is learning to recognize change talk and then reinforcing it. Your goal is to engage the students in the process of change, help them realize how life might be better for them, and how they can make choices to make it better. You don't have to convince a person to make a transformation—ultimately only the students can argue for change and persuade themselves to improve.

Here is the typical mental script I refer back to when I begin a conversation: when in doubt, I can always rely on these questions and statements during an interaction:

- Tell me about your drinking habits (I want to know about quantity and frequency here).

- What is good about your drinking, and what is bad about your drinking?

- Tell me about a time when your drinking has gotten you in trouble or caused you problems.

- On a scale of 1-10, how important is it to you to make this change?

- On a scale of 1-10, how confident are you that you can make this change?

- What will or can you do in the next week to make this change?

Those last few questions are part of the Readiness Ruler,[2] which was developed by Rollnick. It is a

---

[2] Walters and Baer. *Talking with College Students About Alcohol.* 2006.

simple method for determining a person's readiness to change by asking where he or she are on a scale of 1 to 10. The lower numbers show less readiness, and the higher numbers signify greater readiness for change. Depending on how ready a student thinks he are to change, the conversation can take different directions. I really like the flexibility of these questions. No matter the response/number the student picks, it gives you something to work with. It is easy to take that answer and keep moving forward. Even if you have an answer of "1" (the lowest), you can still work with that!

If the student gives you a very low number like a 1, use a simple question, asking what it would take to raise the number a few spots. Or, specifically ask, "What would a 5 look like?" Middle responses give you a few more options. You can reflect back and ask why he chose that middle number and not a one. This will elicit the student's motivations for changing which can then be reflected on and strengthened. Another option for middle responses is to stay forward focused, asking about raising the number. When a student gives a higher number response, this signifies a much higher motivation to change, and it is time to move toward commitment. Respond with open-ended and forward-focused questions such as, "What would the change look like to you?"

One evening while I was walking foot patrol, I came across a couple of students who were cutting through the north quad, near the local drinking establishments. When I addressed them with a, "Hi guys, how's it going?" and they responded with a quick, "Hey!" I could tell that they hadn't recognized that I was a police officer, in full uniform no less! Their faces registered surprise, as they quickly tried to conceal open beer cans behind their backs. Now, I'm sure you are all familiar with this "smooth move" that works every time (not). We stopped and had a conversation—I did not need to point out that they were in the wrong; their body language let me know that they already knew that.

I didn't take a hard approach in my communication; I used the MI approach. They clearly had started drinking before going to the bars. This made it easy to ask how much alcohol they had already consumed. I then asked them how frequently they drank. To lighten the mood so it didn't feel like an interrogation, I guided the conversation to talk about some of the good things about drinking. We then switched gears and reflected on the not-so-good things about drinking. The fact that I asked about the good things caught them off guard and helped lower their resistance. A police officer having a conversation with students about the good things related to drinking tends to surprise students.

Then asking about the negative aspects of drinking got them to really think about their drinking habits.

The "A-HA" moment…. I asked, "I'm wondering, what do you make of all this?"

One student said, "I don't know, it just seems like I've got to do something about my drinking. I never thought of myself as an extreme drinker. I just figured I drank as much as everyone else and it is normal. But yeah, it is really hurting my grades and my parents would be so mad if I got kicked out! I'm the first kid in my family to go to college."

I then asked where that leaves them now.

The student replied, "I'm going to not drink as much and only on the weekends so I can study during the week."

From my own personal experience, I love helping the students realize that they have the power within themselves to change. It is a great feeling to see the light bulb go off and witness an "A-HA" moment.

SECTION V

Many of the skills you have learned and the experiences you've had as a police officer will apply to motivational interviewing. I'm talking about how you've most likely already developed a thick skin and don't take things (too) personally. The MI tools will continue to help you roll with resistance and keep things moving forward.

As you've seen, MI combines a set of skills and strategies mixed with principles of collaboration. Just like police work, it's more than just a set of techniques — it's a way of being. The final outcome will be a result of the joint effort between you and the students you interact with. In true MI style, change is always constant!

As a campus police officer, you often have to deal with resistance. With motivational inter-viewing, I encourage you to see this resistance in a new, more constructive light — any resistance you may encounter simply means that the person views the situation differently than you do. This will allow you to understand his perspective and move forward from there. When you see resistance as an opportunity to respond in a different way, it helps you to keep your cool and allows you to take advantage of the situation without becoming confrontational.

Sustain Talk

I want to take a brief minute here to unpack what "resistance" means in MI. I know you are familiar with the term "resistance" in terms of use of force. Although the MI phrase for resistance are "sustain talk and discord,"[1] I prefer to stick to "resistance." Based on your training, this is what it will look and feel like.

As police officers, you are used to someone arguing with you, interrupting, ignoring, or even discounting you. Paired with MI, your current training will be even more effective against this resistance. In MI this type of resistance is called discord.

Another kind of resistance you will experience using MI is sustain talk. You will be working with a student using MI hoping to help them go from point A to point B. If the student voices reasons to not go and not make a change it will look and feel like resistance. Sustain talk is normal when working with change. Think of it as weighing the pros and cons of making a change. This is where MI focuses on the ambivalence of change. You will

---

[1] Miller, William R., and Stephen Rollnick. Motivational Interviewing: Helping People Change. 3rd ed. New York, NY: Guilford Press, 2013.

use the MI skills to explore this ambivalence and help the student resolve it; hopefully moving towards making positive changes. In the next section we will discuss ways to roll with resistance (read: sustain talk).

Rolling with Resistance

I'm sure you've had the experience of dealing with a person who refuses to acknowledge that a problem exists. You may even have been in a situation or two where you've personally felt the same way. When you are feeling under attack or feeling criticized, denial is a very natural defensive response. The term "rolling with resistance" refers to how to deal with someone who is at one of two extremes. Either the individual disappears into his or her shell or is very confrontational. Here's where your cop training and MI will mesh well to help you work through resistance. The key is that you roll with resistance; don't oppose it. You want to help maintain the momentum toward change by:

- Listening reflectively

- Re-framing or simply changing tactics

- Acknowledging resistance as understandable

Here's an example of a conversation where a student began to give some resistance and seemed to reject every idea or suggestion I had:

Student: I don't want to stop drinking.

Me: You're right. What you choose to do is your business. You could quit, cut back, keep on as you are, or drink even more if you want.

My goal was to keep the conversation going and to remind this person that he was in charge of deciding on his own how to address the problem. In my experience, the instant feedback you get from MI is one of the best ways to roll with resistance. Remember that MI is just one of the tools you have to use. The spirit of MI is that the technique carries the momentum — if you have to force it or if it doesn't work, just switch to another tool.

Traps to Avoid

Your goals for a student and a student's objectives may not always align. As you've no doubt already experienced (and as I highlighted in the section on How and Why People Change), trying to get someone to change can be a frustrating experience. If individuals feel coerced, it may make them less likely to change. I would venture to add that the greater your personal investment in a particular outcome, the more inappropriate it is to use MI. Everyone has a choice—no matter what you say, the decision is ultimately up to the individual. The more you understand this, the less personal it becomes if someone makes a different choice or makes a poor decision.

Here are a few of the common traps you may come across:

Question-Answer Trap — Because of the need for specific information, it can be easy to get caught up in asking too many questions—especially those questions that can be answered with a simple "yes" or "no." This may make the students feel defensive, as if they are being interrogated. Or it can put them in a passive position, where they feel no sense of self efficacy in the process. Be sure to use reflections between asking questions to avoid this trap.

Premature Focus Trap — You may see an issue that needs to be immediately resolved, but that might not line up with the student's point of view. If you can start with the issue that aligns with the student's main concern, you will reduce resistance. By moving the conversation forward, you can eventually bring the perspective back to what concerns you.

Confrontation Trap — When you confront or clash with the person by taking the opposite side of an issue, it may produce defensiveness or allow him to talk himself out of change. Reflections and re-frames of what the person is saying can help you avoid this trap. By making the student argue both sides, it allows for the collaborative spirit of MI, rather than pitting the student against you.

Blame Game Trap — You may find that a student is overly concerned with who is to blame for their problems. This can leave you in an endless circle, draining your energy and wasting time. Reassure the person that the goal is not to assign blame, but to find a solution for the current situation. You can then use your redirect techniques to shift attention away from playing the blame game.

Expert Trap — This can happen if you come across as an expert who just wants to fix the person's problem. With MI, the main goal is to guide a person through resolving ambivalence. At its best,

MI is always about collaborating with someone, not solving the problem for them.

Given that your goal when working with individuals is behavior change (whatever that behavior may be), you have a choice about which kind of interactive atmosphere you want to create. With MI, the interaction between you and the student will produce an atmosphere that either facilitates change (using OARS) or that discourages change (falling into traps).

Dual Role – Enforcement and Motivational Interviewing

> *Sometimes we have to just step up and be the police.*

When your job is to preserve the peace and protect the public, you have the power to influence a person's choices or the outcome of those choices. In dealing with students, you must play two conflicting roles — a representative of the college to enforce the laws and a counselor/educator (sometimes feels like a babysitter) for the students. Here are a few ways in which you can navigate this dual role of patrolling for compliance while at the same time, maintaining a motivational style.

Highlight Your Dual Role

The best course of action is to always be up front with those individuals you come across. Be honest about your role and any conditions or sanctions that may occur when you're on the scene. For example, when I arrived at the room of our favorite pot smoker, not only was I dressed in uniform, I also made it clear that I was responding to a call. After I explained myself, I gave him the opportunity to share anything with me that I needed to know as a campus police officer before we began. While I explored MI with him, I emphasized that after our conversation, he was the one who would be making the choices about his behavior.

Be Clear About any Sanctions

Always make sure that students are aware of what sanctions may occur as a result of a violation. Obviously, it's best to do this when the individual is close to getting a sanction. With motivational interviewing, keep in mind that you're collaborating in order to elicit a change in behavior. Whether you need to give a verbal warning, issue a campus citation or make an arrest (whichever applies to your situation), always ensure that a student is never caught off guard by a sanction.

Stay Calm and Interview On

Of course, you already know that telling someone to "calm down" goes over about as well as a lead balloon, but I do want to emphasize that your attitude really does matter. Blustering or being hostile doesn't work. In fact, it just tends to make a potentially difficult situation even more complicated. If you are agitated, you could make an already defensive person's attitude worse. For this reason, always approach MI with an even temper. Focus on addressing the behavior and if you must,

give out the appropriate sanctions in a way
doesn't agitate the individual.

How to Handle Lying

It's reasonable to expect deception from time to time and to understand that people will "bend the truth" for the simplest (read: dumbest) reasons. Lying and deception are just part of the human experience. A person might lie to cover a bad choice or to hide inner fears or they may not even realize how they are lying to themselves about destructive behavior. So, it isn't so much a matter of whether or not someone will lie to you, it's the degree of deception that you have to evaluate. When you are dealing with MI, the key is to focus on allowing the conversation to keep on moving forward.

To those of you who think MI may not work because the kids will just lie, I'd like to share a couple of interesting things that will happen if you are able to stay calm and interview on. Just like in a regular police interview, when you allow an individual to keep talking, they will eventually talk themselves into a corner and be forced to make a choice. Then bingo, they are caught in the lie! In addition, a fascinating aspect of MI is that when you begin to use OARS, you will take the conversation to a deeper level: asking about feelings, building rapport, and showing empathy. As the student moves through the OARS, they will often have a change of heart about the lies.

How to Use Advice and Feedback

As you've read through this book, you've learned that when it comes to MI, how you present information can affect how it is received. Let's look at some valuable techniques that will allow you to present knowledge in a non-judgmental, neutral and positive way. This will go a long way in empowering a person to make informed decisions about changing a behavior. People you come across on campus may have little or no insight into their behaviors. Traditionally, students are encouraged to quit or change a destructive behavior through advice. Unfortunately, studies have shown that only 5 to 10% of students quit smoking just because they are told smoking is bad for their health. The reason of course, is that most people do not like to be told what to do! As we've discussed, for most of us, change is an inside job.

That's the beauty of MI — it works in conjunction with our natural preference for being given choices while making decisions, especially those that involve changing our behaviors. A frequently used MI strategy is to offer advice or feedback that involves:

- Providing feedback that allows an individual to compare their behavior to that of others so they know how their behavior relates and where they stand. Presenting personalized feedback in a motivational manner will allow a person to evaluate the feedback you've given. They can then see how relevant it is to their own lives. "I guess I drink as much as my friends, but maybe we are all drinking more than we should."

- Asking the students what they know about how their risky behavior affects other aspects of their life. If they're unsure, you can step in with one or two brief facts. This can then be followed up by asking if they'd like to learn even more, and then be prepared to give them material that you have prepared or made available.

- Focusing on the positives of changing. Many people may not be aware of the benefits of giving up drinking or smoking, for example. Be prepared to have current information to share.

Here are a few examples of how you can provide feedback during a conversation. It typically begins with asking if you can talk about the person's behavior:

"Do you mind if we spend a few minutes talking about____?" You could follow this up with, "What do you know about____?"

"What do you know about how your drinking affects your _____?" You could fill in the blank with whichever is appropriate (such as studies /relationships/family).

"What do you know about the laws, and what will happen if you get a second drunk driving arrest?" (Or similar sanction for a particular behavior).

"You said that you know the legal limit for drunk driving is 0.08%. What do you know about how many drinks it takes to get to that level?"

Did you notice anything about the examples above? Well, let's look at it a little differently, and because we in law enforcement are such fans of acronyms, we will use another: E-P-E.[2] This lovely advice giving acronym stands for Elicit - Provide - Elicit. Beginning with eliciting information is a very important step, as it shows respect and ensures you don't tell them anything they already know. Think about when someone has tried to give you advice about something you already know. You instantly tune out, rather than list. By

[2] *Motivational Interventions for College Drinkers*. Illinois Higher Education Center for Alcohol, Other Drug and Violence Prevention, 2015.

eliciting before moving to the second step, which is providing advice, you are setting yourself and your advice up for success. The third step in E-P-E, is elicit. This step is what seals the deal by ensuring the advice was understood correctly. It also serves as a great chance for reflective listening. This step will keep you from falling into the "expert trap" that we previously discussed and will continue to keep the student engaged in the conversation.

Offering advice and asking permission is a great way to set MI out in front of someone and then step back and let it unfold! You will be surprised by the ideas people come up with when given the opportunity. One of the best things about MI, in my opinion, is that when an individual finds success in one area, they will often apply what they've learned in other areas of their life.

WRAP UP

Motivational interviewing is a highly rewarding method for working with people to change their lives for the better. It really does work! Remember that to get it right will take a lot of practice and reflection on your sessions, especially in the beginning. It can be very easy to forget specific techniques, so refer back to this book often and keep up your interactions.

Even if you only have one chance, with MI you can:

- Help a person find a new perspective and see what barriers to move

- Engage with a person in such a way that it allows them to see you as a resource for change

- Encourage a student to make a first step toward change

- Help them develop a first step to a new life

I have personally found that MI actually makes engaging with even the most difficult and challenging individual a lot less difficult than any other method I have used. When you step back and hand over the reins to these students, their capacity for change will surprise and inspire you.

With MI you can properly guide them, allowing them to harness their inner potential to shine and ultimately help them change for the better.

The most powerful motivators in life are fundamental — your family, friends and feeling a measure of control over your life. These are the driving forces you will tap into when you use MI. Remember that the goal here when you interact with individuals is not to get enough information to fill out a report but to motivate a person to change.

When you read through this book and put what you've learned into practice, you are in the business of motivation! You never know where the small actions you put into motion can lead — the momentum to change begins with you! Now go ahead and take the first step...

OARS EXAMPLES

Open Ended Questions

What concerns do you have about ___?

How has ____ caused trouble for you?

What are some good things about ____?

What are some not so good things about ____?

What do you think would happen if you don't make a change?

How would you want your life to be different in, say, 5 years?

What worked for you in the past?

How can you make that happen?

What things might get in the way?

What's that like for you?

What else?

Who would help you?

Affirmations

Thanks for talking with me.

Thanks for telling me about that.

It's clear you have thought about this a lot.

You care a lot about your health.

You have a lot of leadership qualities and I bet people look up to you.

I appreciate your honesty.

Reflections

It is frustrating to you.

It makes you angry.

It feels like it might be a waste of time, and so it frustrates you.

It feels like there are no good options here.

It's difficult to be around your friends and not drink.

It doesn't seem to you like it's causing you any problems.

Summaries

Let me see if I understand so far...

Here is what I've heard. Tell me if I've missed anything.

Did I hear you correctly?

We covered that well. Now let's talk about...

MI FROM START TO FINISH

Officer: I really appreciate you opening the door to speak with me. [Affirmation]

Student: Well, it's not like I had much of a choice. I don't want to get kicked out of school.

Officer: Yeah, I understand that. Still, it is great that you are talking with me. It is never fun when the police show up at your door on a Friday night. [Affirmation]

Student: No kidding.

Officer: Let me tell you why we are here. We received a report of loud music and partying. I do see that there has been some drinking going on. I'd like to talk about that.

Student: It wasn't my fault! We are just hanging out listening to music and having a couple of drinks. I have only had 2!

Officer: So it seems unfair that we are here. [Reflection]

Student: Yeah this campus has robberies and rapes every year and I get busted for 2 beers.

Officer: It seems to you like we should be

spending our time on other things. [Reflection]

Student: Yeah, this campus sucks.

Officer: Okay, we have to be here addressing the complaint even though it's not what you'd like us to be doing. It actually pisses you off a little. So I'm wondering, since we have to be here, what could we talk about that would help you? [Open-ended question]

Student: I don't know.

Officer: Tell me a little bit about your drinking. [Open-ended question]

Student: I don't drink that much, mainly on the weekend.

Officer: Mostly on the weekends. [Reflection]

Student: Yeah, when I get together with my friends.

Officer: Drinking is a social thing for you. [Reflection]

Student: Yes, I can't stop drinking because then I wouldn't have any friends to hang out with.

Officer: So mostly with friends on the weekends. When you do drink, about how many drinks do you have?

Student: Maybe 6 to 8 beers.

Officer: Other than us being here tonight, tell me about a time drinking has caused a problem for you. [Open-ended question]

Student: I don't know. Do you mean like blacking out?

Officer: Sure.

Student: I guess I did black out the other weekend.

Officer: What was that like for you? [Open-ended question]

Student: Well, I'm not really sure what happened. My friends said I was a fool.

Officer: It was embarrassing for you. [Reflection]

Student: Kind of. I mean something bad could have happened and I wouldn't even know.

Officer: A little scary to you. [Reflection]

Student: Yeah, I should probably cut back on my drinking so that doesn't happen again.

Officer: Not knowing what happened that night worries you. If you did decide to cut back on drinking, what would that look like? [Reflection]

[Open-ended question]

Student: I wouldn't take shots any more. Those always seem to put me over the line.

Officer: What else? [Open-ended question]

Student: I would maybe pace my drinks and always make sure I am with my friends.

Officer: On a scale of 1 to 10, how important is it to you to make a change in your drinking?

Student: Maybe a 6.

Officer: That is interesting you said a 6 and not a 1 or 2. What made you pick 6? [Open-ended question]

Student: I don't know. Kind of like I already told you. It is embarrassing and scary when I black out. I don't want anything bad to happen to me.

Officer: What would it take to raise it from a 6 to say, an 8? [Open ended question]

Student: Well, getting caught by the police tonight might bump it to an 8.

Officer: You've already started thinking about making a change. [Reflection]

Student: Yeah, between blacking out and now

getting caught, seems like I might be headed down the wrong road.

Officer: You want to make a change before something really bad happens.

Student: Yes, I don't want to get hurt or kicked out of school.

Officer: Well, using that same scale of 1 to10, how confident are you that you could make a change? [Open-ended question]

Student: An 8.

Officer: You are quite confident. How will you go about it? [Open-ended question]

Student: I am going to stick to beer. Saying no to shots.

Officer: What else? [Open-ended question]

Student: I will set a limit of 4 to 5 drinks when I go out.

Officer: I think your plans to avoid shots and limit your drinks will really help you out. You have really put some thought into this. [Affirmation]

Student: I don't want anything bad to happen.

Officer: Me either. Thank you again for being honest and taking time to talk with me.

Student: Sure.

PRACTICE TIPS

Experiment One

Here is one way to get a feel for the MI style. Grab a friend and try this experiment.

Think about something you want to change, need to change or should change. Instruct your friend to be the "helper" as you have a conversation about this thing you want to change. Share the topic with the helper. Then let them tell you how much you need to make this change, give you a list of reasons to make the change and then tell you how to make the change.

How did that conversation make you feel? Uncomfortable, angry, defensive, or powerless?

Now using the same topic, instruct the helper to ask you open-ended questions. After each question your friend (helper) will give you a brief summary of what you said.

"What is driving you to make the change?"
"What else?"

"How might you go about it in order to succeed?"

"What are the top 3 reasons to make this change?"

"How important is it for you to make this change?"

"What do you think you will do?"

Reflect on that conversation. Did it leave you feeling understood, open, and empowered?

The questions aren't where the power comes from; it comes from the style of the interaction.

Experiment Two

Reflections are the key to making MI work. The best MI practice advice I can give you is to use more reflections. The ability of reflections to move a conversation to a deeper level can be used in any conversation. You can start practicing MI by using reflections in everyday conversations. The next time you are talking to your wife, husband, significant other, child or friend, give it a try. One simple reflection can make a world of difference in a conversation. Just as a refresher, here are the three types of reflections.

- Repeating/rephrasing: Repeat or rephrase what the speaker has said, staying close to the original statements.

- Paraphrasing: Create a new statement in which the speaker's intention is implied.

- Reflection of feeling: Emphasize the emotional aspects of the conversation.

ROLE-PLAY GUIDES

Scenario 1

Mike Jones: 19-year-old freshman

Issue: Has 3 individuals in his residence hall room; loud music complaint. All individuals have had a few beers.

Additional Information: Mike was transported to the local hospital the previous weekend for incapacitation due to alcohol. Had a BAC of 0.24 that weekend.

Mike Reports:

   Had a few drinks that weekend but doesn't remember how many.

   Parties on most Thursdays, Fridays, and Saturdays. Drinks with friends and generally has an average of 10 drinks per night.

Student Role Player: Exhibit low resistance to MI. After initial discussion, relate the cause of the negative consequences of drinking alcohol.

Scenario 2

Michelle Smith: 21-year-old senior

Issue: Open container on the campus quad.

Additional Information: Michelle has had previous alcohol-related incidents with campus police.

Michelle Reports:

>   Uses alcohol to relieve stress and relax.

>   Drinks most days.

Student Role Player: Show mild to moderate resistance. Exhibit mild depression and feelings of isolation.

Scenario 3

Brad Styles: 20-year-old sophomore

Issue: Smoking cannabis in his residence hall room.

Additional Information: Brad has noticed his grades are dropping to the point where professors have spoken to him, asking if things were okay.

Brad Reports:

> He smokes when he gets stressed out.

> When he smokes he finds it hard to focus on his homework.

Student Role Player: Show moderate amount of resistance. Not sure you want to stop smoking because it relaxes you.

REFERENCES

Agostinelli, Gina, Janice M. Brown, and William R. Miller. "Effects of Normative Feedback on Consumption among Heavy Drinking College Students." Journal of Drug Education, 1995, 31-40.

Bein, Thomas H., William R. Miller, and Joseph M. Boroughs. "Motivational Interviewing with Alcohol Outpatients." Behav. Psychother. Behavioural Psychotherapy, 1993, 347.

Branscum, Paul, and Manoj Sharma. "A Review of Motivational Interviewing-Based Interventions Targeting Problematic Drinking Among College Students." Alcoholism Treatment Quarterly, 2010, 63-77.

Carnegie, Dale. How to Win Friends & Influence People. Rev. ed. New York: Pocket Books, 1998.

"College Drinking." National Institute on Alcohol Abuse and Alcoholism. 2015. Accessed January 7, 2015.

D'amico, Elizabeth J., Karen Chan Osilla, and Sarah B. Hunter. "Developing a Group Motivational Interviewing Intervention for First-Time Adolescent Offenders At-Risk for an Alcohol or Drug Use Disorder." Alcoholism Treatment Quarterly, 2008, 417-36.

Devos-Comby, Loraine, and James E. Lange. "Standardized Measures of Alcohol-related Problems: A Review of Their Use among College Students." Psychology of Addictive

Behaviors, 2008, 349-61.

Dimeff, Linda A. Brief Alcohol Screening and
Intervention for College Students (BASICS): A
Harm Reduction Approach. New York:
Guilford Press, 1999.

Fernandes, Simone, Maristela Ferigolo, Mariana
Canellas Benchaya, Taís De Campos Moreira,
Pollianna Sangalli Pierozan, Cláudia Galvão
Mazoni, and Helena Maria Tannhauser
Barros. "Brief Motivational Intervention and
Telemedicine: A New Perspective of
Treatment to Marijuana Users." Addictive
Behaviors, 2010, 750-55.

Kazemi, Donna M., Maureen J. Levine, Jacek
Dmochowski, Mary A. Nies, and Linman
Sun. "Effects of Motivational Interviewing
Intervention on Blackouts Among College
Freshmen." Journal Of Nursing Scholarship,
2013.

King, Sylvie, and Mariann Suarez. Motivational
Interviewing with Adolescents and Young
Adults. New York: Guilford Press, 2011.

Larimer, M E, A P Turner, B K Anderson, J S Fader, J
R Kilmer, R S Palmer, and J M Cronce.
"Evaluating a Brief Alcohol Intervention with
Fraternities." Journal of Studies on Alcohol J.
Stud. Alcohol, 2001, 370-80.

Maddock, Jason E, Robert G Laforge, Joseph S Rossi,
and Thomas O'hare. "The College Alcohol
Problems Scale." Addictive Behaviors, 2001,
385-98.

Miller, William R., R. Gayle Sovereign, and Barbara
Krege. "Motivational Interviewing with

Problem Drinkers: II. The Drinker's Check-up as a Preventive Intervention." Behav. Psychother. Behavioural Psychotherapy, 1988, 251.

Miller, William R. Motivational Enhancement Therapy Manual: A Clinical Research Guide for Therapists Treating Individuals with Alcohol Abuse and Dependence. Rockville, Md. (6000 Executive Blvd., Rockville 20892-7003): U.S. Dept. of Health and Human Services, Public Health Service, National Institutes of Health, National Institute on Alcohol Abuse and Alcoholism, 1995.

Miller, William R., and Stephen Rollnick. Motivational Interviewing: Helping People Change. 3rd ed. New York, NY: Guilford Press, 2013.

Motivational Interviewing. Guilford Press, 2013. DVD.

Motivational Interventions for College Drinkers. Illinois Higher Education Center for Alcohol, Other Drug and Violence Prevention, 2015. DVD.

Prochaska, James, and WF Velicer. "The Transtheoretical Model of Health Behavior Change." The Science of Health Promotion 12, no. 1 (1997): 38-48.

Quinn, Patrick D., and Kim Fromme. "Alcohol Use and Related Problems Among College Students and Their Noncollege Peers: The Competing Roles of Personality and Peer Influence*." J. Stud. Alcohol Drugs Journal of Studies on Alcohol and Drugs, 2011, 622-32.

Thompson, George J., and Jerry B. Jenkins. Verbal
     Judo: The Gentle Art of Persuasion. Rev. ed.
     New York: Quill, 2004.
Turner, James C, Jennifer Bauerle, and Jianfen Shu.
     "Estimated Blood Alcohol Concentration
     Correlation with Self-reported Negative
     Consequences among College Students Using
     Alcohol." Journal of Studies on Alcohol J.
     Stud. Alcohol, 2006, 741-49.
Walters, Scott T., and John Samuel Baer. Talking with
     College Students about Alcohol: Motivational
     Strategies for Reducing Abuse. New York:
     Guilford Press, 2006.
Walters, Scott T. Motivating Offenders to Change a
     Guide for Probation and Parole. Washington,
     DC: U.S. Dept. of Justice, National Institute of
     Corrections, 2007.
Maximizing Brief Interventions for College Drinkers
     with Dr. Scott Walters. Illinois Higher
     Education Center for Alcohol, Other Drug
     and Violence Prevention, 2011. DVD.